Cody's Lucky Cap

by Milo Jones
illustrated by Paige Billin-Frye

SCHOLASTIC INC.

New York • Toronto • London • Auckland
Sydney • Mexico City • New Delhi • Hong Kong

ISBN 978-0-545-68602-0

Copyright © 2010 by Lefty's Editorial Services.

All rights reserved. Published by Scholastic Inc.

SCHOLASTIC, LET'S LEARN READERS™, and associated logos
are trademarks and/or registered trademarks of Scholastic Inc.

12 11 10 9 8 7 6 5 4 3 2   14 15 16 17 18 19/0

Printed in China.

Cody always hung his lucky cap in the same spot. But one day, he reached for the cap and it was not there.

Take a look at Cody. How do you think he feels?

Uh-oh! Cody was supposed to go fishing with his dad today. How could he catch fish without his lucky cap?

Cody looked under his bed. He looked behind the couch. He even looked in the bathtub. But his lucky cap was nowhere to be found.

QUESTION

Is the bathtub a smart or silly place to look for a cap?

Next Cody asked his family if they had
seen it.

"No, dear," said his mom.

"Sorry, son," said his dad.

But his little brother, Timmy, said nothing.
He hardly knew any words at all.

Where could the lucky cap be? Cody decided to visit all of the places he'd gone yesterday to see if he could find it.

What does Cody's note say?

Cody had gone to the corner store yesterday. The cap was not there. But Cody did find a dollar on the sidewalk. That sure was lucky!

QUESTION

Did Cody find what he was looking for at the corner store?

Cody had gone to his grandma's house yesterday. The cap was not there. But his grandma had just baked a cherry pie. That sure was lucky!

Cody had gone to the playground yesterday. The cap was not there. But his pal Dave let Cody ride on his new pogo stick. That sure was lucky!

Cody had gone to his friend Ann's house yesterday. The cap was not there. But a beautiful butterfly landed right on his shoulder. That sure was lucky!

 CONNECT

Did something lucky ever happen to you? What?

Cody had gone to every place that he had been yesterday. His lucky cap was nowhere to be found. So he decided to go back home.

When Cody opened the front door, he got a big surprise. Timmy was wearing his lucky cap!

"We found it in Timmy's toy box," said his mom.

QUESTION **How do you think Cody's cap might have ended up in Timmy's toy box?**

Cody smiled. He'd had a great day so far. Maybe he didn't need the cap to be lucky after all.

"Timmy," said Cody, "do you want to keep my cap?"

"Yes!" replied Timmy.

"Wow, looks like your little brother just learned a new word," said his dad.

Then Cody and his dad went fishing and had lots and lots of luck.

TIE UP

What lesson did Cody learn in this story?

Story Prompts

Answer these questions after you have read the book.

1 Do you think Cody's cap really was lucky? Why or why not?

2 Do you have a special item of clothing that you would hate to lose? If so, what is it?

3 What lucky things could happen on a fishing trip? Turn on your imagination and tell a story about some!